The Totally U
Guide to Fishing™

A Funny Fishing Book for the Fisherman
Who Has Everything (Except Talent & Fish)

Ricky Woods

Copyright © 2025 Ricky Woods

Published by: Bemberton Ltd

All rights reserved. No part of this book or any portion thereof may be reproduced in any form by any electronic or mechanical means, without permission in writing from the publisher, except for the use of brief quotes in a book review.

The publisher accepts no legal responsibility for any action taken by the reader, including but not limited to financial losses or damages, both directly or indirectly incurred as a result of the content in this book.

ISBN: 978-1-915833-93-8

Disclaimer: The information in this book is general and designed to be for information only. While every effort has been made to ensure it is wholly accurate and complete, it is for general information only. It is not intended, nor should it be taken as professional advice. The author gives no warranties or undertakings whatsoever concerning the content.

The Totally Useless Guide to is a trademark of Bemberton Ltd.

View all our books at **bemberton.com**

CONTENTS

5   Introduction

9   **Chapter 1.** Classic Excuses for Not Catching Anything

19   **Chapter 2.** The Real Meanings Behind Fishing Phrases

33   **Chapter 3.** A Guide to Talking Sh*t at the Lake

43   **Chapter 4.** Fishing Gear You Totally Need (But Definitely Don't)

55   **Chapter 5.** The Cast of Fishing Characters (a.k.a. People You'll Regret Inviting)

73   **Chapter 6.** The Psychology of the Fisherman

85   **Chapter 7.** The Fish Are Laughing At You

95   **Chapter 8.** The Evolution of the Fisherman (In Four Painful Stages)

105   **Chapter 9.** Fishing Bucket List (That You'll Never Complete)

115   **Chapter 10.** Final Cast: What It's *Really* All About

123   Conclusion

INTRODUCTION

It's hard to think of a hobby that has a better reputation than fishing. On paper, it's seen as a peaceful, relaxing hobby. A way to spend time outdoors, quietly perfecting your technique to land the biggest fish in the lake. What could possibly be a better way to spend your time?

As it turns out, just about anything would serve you better than this hopeless, hapless endeavor.

The reputation that fishing holds is total bullsh*t. What's worse is that you already know better. You *know* it's not all it's cracked up to be — but you go along with it anyway. Which means you, my friend, are part of the problem.

A HOBBY BUILT ON LIES

Everyone knows fishermen like to stretch the truth a little. That 20-inch bass they bragged about? More like 18. Or 12. Those lies are silly, but at the end of the day, they don't really matter. Exaggerating the size of a fish by a few inches is a victimless crime.

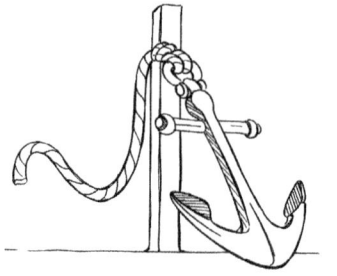

But that's only where it starts.

From there, the stories get bolder. Suddenly, the fisherman is talking about fighting off a bear with one hand while reeling in a record catch with the other. There's something about spending hours alone on the water that melts the brain just enough to create full-blown fishing fan fiction.

And it's not just about the catches. Oh no—fishermen lie about the experience, too. Ask them why they fish, and they'll tell you it's about peace. Tranquility. Zen. They'll talk about rising above the noise of life and connecting with something deeper.

Right.

If fishing were so peaceful, why do you hear so many four-letter words echoing across the lake? For most folks, frustration bubbles just under the surface, ready to explode the moment a line tangles or a cast goes sideways.

Fishing is many things. But calming? That's one hell of a stretch.

LET'S BREAK IT ALL DOWN

The chapters that follow are going to cut through the bull and tell you the real story. The one you might have been avoiding. The one that hits a little too close to home.

But stick with it. Consider this your therapy session. In a weird way, you might just feel better about fishing—and maybe even life—by the time it's over.

CLASSIC EXCUSES FOR NOT CATCHING ANYTHING

1

Trolling: A technique where you drag your lure behind a moving boat. Also describes what your buddy's doing when he tells you fish actually live in this lake.

If you spend enough time around fishermen — arguably too much time — they start to give off some serious "the dog ate my homework" energy.

In other words, it's never their fault.

No matter how many times the boat pulls back into the dock — or the folding chair gets packed up onshore with zero bites to show for hours of wasted time — it's never their fault.

So if this total failure wasn't due to a sheer lack of skill, knowledge, or focus... who is to blame? Funny you should ask, because we're going to dive deep into that question. As it turns out, literally everyone and everything is responsible for the sh***y fishing performance — except, of course, the actual fisherman.

Naturally, you'd never make these excuses yourself. You just hear them from other people. Obviously.

A CONSPIRACY OF NATURE

Fishermen have a complicated relationship with nature. On one hand, they love it. Being outside is one of the best parts of fishing. Whether you're out on a boat, parked in a folding chair by a lake, or balanced on a slippery riverbank with mud in your boots, there's something peaceful about the fresh air, the warm sun, and the quiet promise of a bite.

At the same time, nature is the number one target for excuses when things go wrong. If the fish aren't biting, then nature is likely to blame.

To hear fishermen tell it, you would think that Mother Nature was operating a massive conspiracy to keep as many fish in the water — and out of their nets — as possible. From the outside, this seems ridiculous. To the ones holding a pole, it seems as obvious as could be. Nature has sided with the fish, and that's the end of it.

The excuses in this category are endless. Here's just a small sample:

- "The water's too clear. They can see the hook."

- "The water's too cloudy. They can't see the bait."

- "Full moon. New moon. Wrong moon."

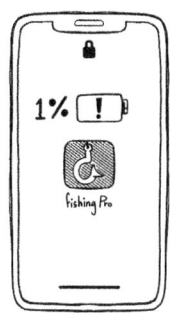

- "This wind is spooking the fish. They can hear the leaves!"
- "I don't care that this is a lake — it's still the wrong tide."
- "The water's too cold. The fish are freezing and sulking."

Apparently, the only acceptable fishing conditions exist in some parallel universe none of us can afford to travel to.

FISHING GEAR FAILURES

There's no shortage of gadgets and gizmos in the world of fishing. While some keep it simple — just a rod, a reel, and a few lures — others dive headfirst into the gear game. They load up their tackle boxes (and their boats) with everything short of sonar and a small submarine. Then, of course, when things go wrong, the culprit is obvious: it's all that sh*t.

Of all the excuses in fishing, gear-related ones are some of the funniest. The fisherman has complete control over what gear they bring. So when they blame it, they're basically blaming themselves — but somehow, they don't see it that way.

Let's explore the gear excuses from fishermen who were totally about to catch a monster... until their rod, reel, or hook conveniently failed at the last second.

- "These hooks aren't sharp enough. They're just snacking and swimming away."

- "This is great gear — it just takes a while to break in. You'll see next trip."
- "The factory didn't clean this gear. The fish smell the humans on it."
- "I was handling that fish perfectly, but this crappy line snapped because it wasn't tested correctly."
- "This rod isn't strong enough for the monsters I usually pull in."
- "Why's this reel so slow? Probably wasn't oiled. Typical."
- "This net has holes in it. I had one in there, and it just swam right through like it was doing laps."
- "Who designed these lures? They don't attract fish. They scare 'em away!"
- "I packed the wrong gear. This setup's for trout and I'm fishing bass."

OTHER DAMN PEOPLE

These are the types of excuses that pretty much everyone can relate to. In life, away from the lake or river, most excuses eventually boil down to blaming somebody else. It just feels good, honestly. You get to give yourself a break and decide that someone else — clearly the idiot — is responsible for whatever went wrong.

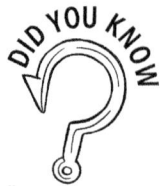

Carp can live for more than 20 years. That's probably longer than your last two marriages!

Given how much fishermen love making excuses, it's no surprise that blaming other people is a top-tier tactic. And on a busy lake or along a crowded shoreline, there's no shortage of targets. Boats, kids, talkers, laughers... they're all getting in the way of your success.

So what kind of behavior ruins a fishing trip? According to the excuse-makers, here's a small sample:

- "That jackass cast his line too close to my boat and scared away all the fish."

- "Those kids throwing rocks from the shore killed everything under the surface."

- "With so many people talking in this boat, how can I concentrate on staring at my line while nothing happens for hours?"

- "I saw a guy in that boat catch a big one. Everyone knows only one decent fish comes out of this lake per day."

- "I think those people up there peed in the river and it floated downstream. Fish hate urine."

- "Why are so many damn boats cruising by and making a wake? The fish are getting dizzy."

- "I knew all the good fishing spots — but while I was eating breakfast, someone stole them."

- "Did I just hear people laughing? Why won't they shut up? There's no laughing at the lake — we're doing serious fishing here!"

- "Someone must've fished here earlier and scared them all off."

Deadstick: A method that involves keeping your bait perfectly still. You probably do this accidentally while wrist-deep in a bag of chips.

WHAT'S WRONG WITH THESE FISH?

A logical person wouldn't blame the fish for coming back to shore with an empty net. After all, you're trying to catch them. Of course, they're going to be elusive. It's a game of cat and mouse — except you're the one with snacks and a hook, and they'd rather not die today.

But logic isn't always a fisherman's strong suit.

Yes, some anglers blame the very fish they're trying to catch for being too smart, too picky, too lazy, or just too damn good at not getting caught. It makes no sense, but that doesn't stop anyone. What are the fish supposed to do — float belly-up and wait to be scooped out like volunteers?

We can all agree that blaming the fish is ridiculous — but it's not going to stop anytime soon. Here's just a sample of how far some fishermen are willing to go:

- "These stupid fish don't eat anymore. I think they've all gone vegan."
- "I'm doing everything right — it's just that the fish in this lake are too small to even take the bait. I'll come back next year."
- "I heard there's a strain of bird flu going through the fish. I think they call it fish flu."
- "Every time I fish shallow, they go deep. Every time I go deep, they stay shallow. It's ridiculous!"
- "It's natural selection. All the dumb fish have been caught. The smart ones survived — and they've gotten even smarter."
- "Why are these fish so picky? Don't they know I'm trying to feed them?"
- "I think the fish here are nocturnal. It's a morning problem."

FLAT OUT MAKING SH*T UP

Most excuses are at least somewhat grounded in reality. Sure, it's childish to blame other people — but those people did make some noise, or take up the good fishing spots. Is it silly to blame the fish? Obviously. But fish are hard to catch. Even when the excuse is dumb, there's usually a sliver of logic behind it.

This last category is different.

This is where the fisherman runs out of options. All the usual excuses have been used. Nature, gear, other people, the fish — nothing's left. No good ideas. No fish. Just desperation.

And that's when the real creativity kicks in.

These excuses aren't even pretending to be true. But that doesn't make them any less entertaining:

- "I had a big one on the line, but a bald eagle swooped down and took it before I could reel it in!"
- "The fish in this lake migrate south for warmer weather each fall. I guess we were a week too late."
- "I caught a bunch today, but let them all go. I wanted to save some for everyone else."
- "I didn't think my boat could handle the weight of the fish I was catching, so I cut the line."

- "I caught so many last time, the warden told me to give the rest of you a chance. They know my reputation."
- "A bear came out of the woods and stole my stringer of fish while I was tying up the boat."
- "I didn't want to peak too early in the season."

And there you have it: nature, gear, strangers, fish, and bald eagles. All working together to sabotage your otherwise flawless fishing performance.

If you haven't caught a single thing, don't worry — you've still got a full tackle box of excuses to fall back on.

THE REAL MEANINGS BEHIND FISHING PHRASES 2

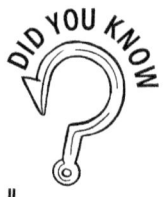

Bass can smell up to 1,000 times better than humans. Keep that in mind next time you hit the lake with beer breath.

For a sport that's supposed to be quiet, there sure is a lot of talking.

Fishermen never shut up.

Sure, they might whisper to avoid "spooking the fish," but they're still talking. (By the way, those fish are underwater, probably hundreds of feet away — and they don't have ears. Are we sure they're even listening?)

Even if the fish could hear, all they'd catch is a steady stream of bullsh*t. Like golf (we're looking at you, golfers), fishing has developed its own secret language where no one says exactly what they mean. Instead, fishermen speak in code.

The good news? This code isn't hard to crack once you know what to listen for.

This chapter is your official translation guide. We'll walk you through common fishing phrases — and what they *actually* mean — broken down by category.

You've definitely heard some of these before. After today, they'll be as clear as a mountain stream on a cold morning.

LIES ABOUT SIZE

This one's a classic. Fishermen love to lie about size.

They're obsessed with talking about how big it was, how much bigger theirs was compared to everyone else's, and how it was the biggest thing they've ever handled.

(We are talking about fish. Obviously.)

Of course, what they say about the size of their fish and what they actually mean are two very different things. Here's your translation key:

- **"It had to be at least ten pounds."**
  It might have been five. Six, tops — if it swallowed a rock.

- **"It bent my pole all the way in half!"**
  I snagged a stump and yanked the rod like a lunatic.

- **"That monster broke my line while I was reeling it in."**
  I never saw the fish — it was probably just a log.

- **"This is the biggest fish I've caught all season."**
  It's *also* the only fish I've caught all season.

- **"You should have seen it!"**
  I'm not going to show you any pictures, so you just have to take my word it.

- **"It ripped the hook right off of my line."**
  I never learned how to tie a proper knot.

- **"That one got wrapped up on the anchor line."**
  We're trolling. There's no anchor.

- **"My arms hurt from reeling it in."**
  I'm out of shape.

- **"It was so big it wouldn't fit in the net."**
  I forgot to bring a net.

- **"It fought so hard it almost pulled me into the water."**
  The only thing that almost pulled me in was losing my balance trying to untangle the line from a branch.

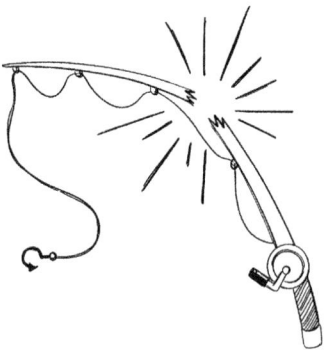

- **"I swear, it snapped my rod clean in half."**
  The rod was already cracked from when I slammed it in the car door last week.

- **"It stripped 300 yards of line before I could even blink!"**
  I forgot to set the drag and it unraveled like a cheap sweater.

- **"I think it was a record-breaker. Easily."**
  Nobody measured anything, and the fish is now safely in the realm of pure imagination.

- **"The fish was so strong, it almost *towed* the boat."**
  The wind pushed the boat. The fish was three pounds, max.

Hookset: Yanking the rod to drive the hook into a fish's mouth — or, more likely, your own hand.

THE PERFECT TECHNIQUE

To hear fishermen tell it, they all have perfect technique. They have mastered the art of fishing and execute their movements correctly time after time. It doesn't matter that they barely practice and spend more time digging through the beer cooler than the tackle box — you're still supposed to believe they are precision-engineered angling machines.

But they aren't. And somewhere, deep down, they know it. So when you hear the statements below, here's what they *really* mean:

- **"I've been doing this for years."**
  I fish twice a year and still have to Google how to tie a knot.

- **"It's all in the wrist."**
  I saw someone do it like this on YouTube once.

- **"You just have to feel it when you cast."**
  I have absolutely no idea what I'm doing.

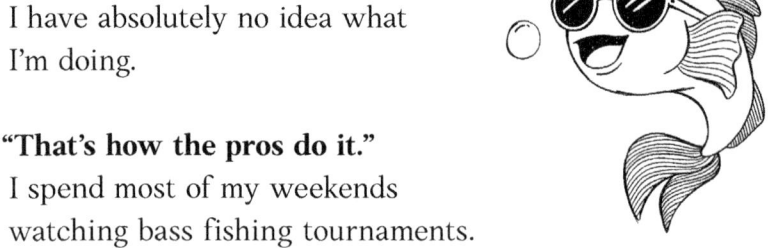

- **"That's how the pros do it."**
  I spend most of my weekends watching bass fishing tournaments.

- **"You gotta work the lure just right while it's underwater."**
  I have no clue why I just got a bite.

- **"Just watch how I do it."**
  Please, fishing gods, let me get lucky while someone's looking.

- **"Set the hook just like this when you get a bite."**
  I just close my eyes and hope for the best.

- **"I learned this from an old-timer around here."**
  If it doesn't work, it's not *my* fault.

- **"I could fish with my eyes closed."**
  And the results would be exactly the same: no fish in the net.

- **"It's muscle memory at this point."**
  It's mostly panic and guesswork if we're being honest.

- **"I was just testing the action on that cast."**
  I wildly overshot and am now pretending I meant to.

- **"I like to keep my rod tip at the perfect angle."**
  I have no idea what the perfect angle is, but saying that makes me sound competent.

- **"That was a practice cast."**
  I hit a tree and now I'm pretending I meant to.

Fish finder: A fancy device that tells you where the fish are. None of which you'll actually catch.

ENVIRONMENTAL CONCERNS

It's funny what fishing does to a person. On the one hand, a day on the lake doesn't exactly scream "environmentally responsible." Firing up a smoky boat motor, dripping oil into the water, and tossing around enough plastic gear to outfit a small landfill doesn't land you on the cover of Eco Warrior Weekly.

Oh — and let's not forget the whole "killing a living thing for fun" part. This isn't exactly the hobby of your typical tree-hugging nature lover.

And yet, somehow, many fishermen magically turn into environmentalists the moment their fishing trip doesn't go as planned. When things go wrong — or just don't go their way — suddenly it's about *conservation*. It's no longer a failed outing. It's a noble, planet-saving mission.

Here are just a few of the "eco excuses" you're likely to hear, along with what they *actually* mean:

- **"I don't like catching fish when they're spawning."**
  I got skunked and needed an excuse.

- **"They shouldn't let so many boats on this lake at one time."**
  The other fishermen are better than me.

- **"The local ecosystem is out of balance due to global warming."**
  I heard someone say that on a podcast once.

- **"I only keep the fish I'm going to eat."**
  I didn't catch anything worth keeping.

- **"Catch and release is the best policy."**
  The only fish I caught was smaller than my bait.

- **"The water in this lake is so much warmer than it used to be."**
  I just peed off the side of the boat.

- **"There are too many invasive species in the water."**
  I have no idea what an invasive species is — or why that's bad.

- **"I don't like overfishing this spot."**
  It's not overfished. I'm just underperforming.

- **"I stopped fishing because the fish looked stressed."**
  I stopped because I got bored and hungry.

- **"We should leave some for the next generation."**
  Let the next generation have 'em. I haven't caught sh*t anyway.

- **"I'm out here to connect with nature, not necessarily to catch fish."**
  I would 100% prefer to catch fish. I'm just pretending this was the plan.

IT'S GOTTA BE THE GEAR

Gear is a huge part of the modern fishing experience. So huge, in fact, that we're dedicating an entire chapter to it later in the book — because there's just so much to say about how fishermen project their failures onto their tools.

For now, let's continue our translation work in this very popular category.

Fishermen spend an incredible amount of time talking about gear — but they're not always being honest. And by "not always," we mean *never*. They are never being honest about their gear or the role it plays in their fishing performance.

So here's your BS-to-English decoder ring for gear talk:

- **"I don't know what's wrong — this lure always works."**
  It caught one fish ten years ago.

- **"Forgot to bring the net on the boat."**
  Left it behind on purpose so I'd have an excuse when nothing bites.

- **"I'm not used to this rod and reel combination just yet."**
  I've been using this setup for years.

- **"This isn't my main gear setup."**
  This is the only gear I own — and I still don't know how to use it.

- **"I think the drag is off on this reel."**
  I don't know what the drag is or how to fix it.

- **"Forgot my lucky lure back at the dock."**
  Feels better blaming luck than skill.

- **"This rod isn't stiff enough for these fish."**
  I couldn't catch them with a 2x4 and a grappling hook.

- **"This line is too visible in the water."**
  There aren't any fish here to see the line anyway.

- **"This reel is too smooth — I can't feel anything."**
  I wouldn't feel a whale if it hit the boat.

- **"I usually use a fluorocarbon leader for this kind of water."**
  I'm just stringing fancy words together to sound like I know stuff.

- **"I'm still adjusting to the gear sensitivity."**
  I bumped the rod holder and dropped my sandwich.

- **"This setup's better for saltwater."**
  This lake has never seen salt and neither have I.

Cold front: A weather shift that ruins your fishing day. Also describes your spouse's mood after you fish all weekend.

KING OF THE LAKE

Fishermen are no strangers to bluster. In fact, they're famous for it. Despite overwhelming evidence to the contrary, every person holding a rod seems to believe they are the greatest angler the world has ever known. And they're not shy about letting others know it.

A lot of the chatter you'll hear around the lake will be self-declared fishing legends holding court. Are they really that confident in their skills? Or are they just projecting insecurity through bravado?

You already know the answer.

Here are just a few of the things you might hear—and what you should actually hear when they land in your ears:

- **"Nobody knows this lake like I do."**
  I fished here once three years ago.

- **"I've taught most of the people at this lake how to fish."**
  They didn't ask me for help, but I gave advice anyway.

- **"I've forgotten more about fishing than you'll ever know."**
  I've also forgotten everything I ever knew.

- **"You should see my wall at home."**
  I have photos of fish other people caught—some of them are from the internet.

- **"Go fishing with me and you'll never go hungry."**
  Because I know a good pizza place near the boat launch.

- **"They call me the fish whisperer."**
  I call me that. No one else ever has.

- **"Everyone around here follows me on Instagram."**
  So they can see where I fish… and go somewhere else.

- **"I catch my limit every time out."**
  I don't even know what the legal limit is on this lake.

- **"I once landed a fish bigger than this boat."**
  It was a perch. A *small* perch.

- **"They should name a dock after me out here."**
  Because I fall off it at least once per season.

- **"I taught my dog to retrieve fish."**
  My dog refuses to go on the boat with me anymore.

- **"I've fished every square foot of this lake."**
  I've been to the same two spots and got lost once.

These translations should help you cut through the B.S. the next time you're out on the water. Fishermen love to talk — but they're rarely telling the truth. Now you'll know who's got your back... and who you might want to throw overboard.

A GUIDE TO TALKING SH*T AT THE LAKE
3

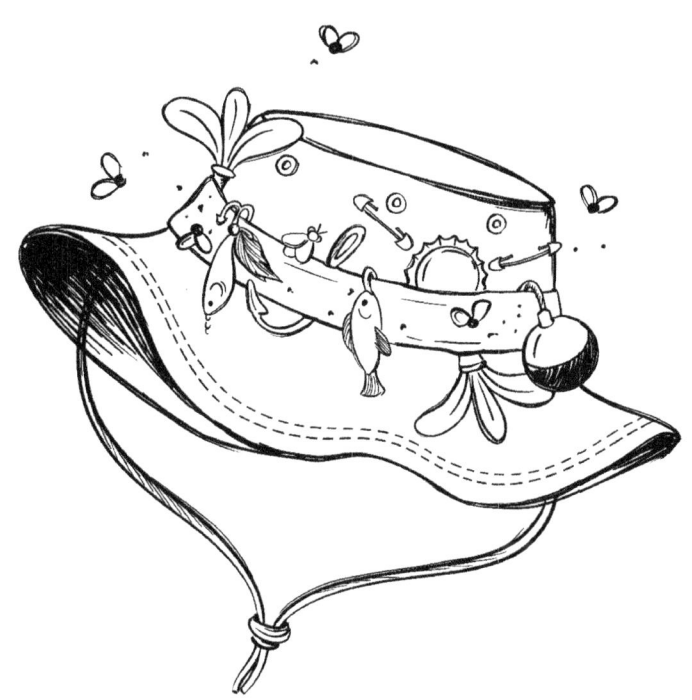

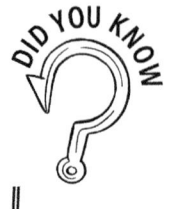

There are over 30,000 known species of fish. How many have you caught? Maybe three?

Let's be honest — most fishing trips aren't really about the fish. Sure, you want to catch a few while you're out on the lake or wading into a river, but what you really want to do is talk sh*t with your friends. If given the choice between landing a monster fish or dropping a line that makes the whole group laugh until they cry, most fishermen will go for the joke.

There's always another fish. But there's only one chance to deliver the perfect burn.

For some people, talking sh*t comes naturally. It's like taking a — well, you get the idea. The ability to trash talk with finesse is a gift. For others, it takes practice. If you're in the second camp, don't worry — this chapter has your back.

STARTER INSULTS

You've got to walk before you run. Or in this case, wade in before you dive deep with the pros.

Don't expect to come out swinging with legendary one-liners right away. Sh*t talking is a craft. It takes confidence, timing, and a few failed attempts to find your style. So start small.

Try a few of these light jabs to test the waters. If one doesn't land, shrug it off and keep casting. Once you get the hang of it, you'll be ready for the more ruthless stuff later in the chapter.

- "If this was a fishing video game, you'd still be on the tutorial."
- "Are you trying to catch fish or scare them away?"
- "Your scorecard is one tangled line, zero fish caught."
- "Your stringer looks like the 'Before' picture in a fishing rod ad."

- "You brought three rods and five tackle boxes — but not a single clue."
- "Are you actually trying to catch fish, or did you just come for Instagram content?"
- "I wouldn't call this fishing — you're just generously feeding worms to the lake."
- "You cast your line like my toddler throws spaghetti."
- "You'd catch the same number of fish in a kiddie pool in your backyard."

- "Fish avoid your line out of pity. They don't want to embarrass you."
- "Nice rod. Shame it didn't come with instructions."
- "The only thing you know how to cast is judgment at other fishermen."
- "You've caught more sunburn than fish today."
- "Even the bait looks embarrassed to be on your hook."
- "I've seen better casting in a school play."

GETTING A LITTLE MORE SERIOUS

Now you've got your legs under you. A few of the lines you dropped on your last trip actually got some laughs, and you started feeling cocky. Then you went in for the kill with a savage line and... nothing. Dead silence. Total miss. And now your confidence is flopping on the dock like a fish that slipped the hook.

Does that mean it's time to give up the trash-talking life and go back to quietly watching your bobber?

Absolutely not.

It means it's time to double down — and turn up the heat.

This section brings out the heavier artillery. These are the kind of lines that can rattle even the most seasoned angler.

- "The only thing you've caught today is shade from my superior skills."
- "You fish like your mom still does your laundry."
- "If your fishing matched your ego, you'd have a full cooler by now."
- "Your rod's seen less action today than your Tinder profile."
- "You've caught more feelings at the bar than fish from this lake."
- "Patience is a virtue. At this point, you might actually be the Pope."
- "Nice new reel — what was it, another YouTube suggestion?"
- "Are you sure you're fishing? From here, it just looks like birdwatching."
- "You've had one bite all day — and I think the fish felt sorry for you."
- "I got my kid a Snoopy rod for his birthday. He could outfish you — and he's two."
- "Those empty beer cans floating in the water have caught more than you today."

- "That line's been sitting in the water so long it's got squatters' rights."

Jigging: A technique that makes bait look like it's nervously dancing in the water. Also your exact movement when you need to pee and can't get to shore.

WHEN SOMEONE CATCHES A FISH

Believe it or not, sometimes — when the stars align and the fish gods are feeling generous — people actually catch something.

Sure, it sounds like a myth, but we've seen it happen. Not often, mind you, but just enough to keep the hope alive.

You might think this is the moment to stop talking sh*t. After all, someone just had success while the rest of you are still staring at motionless bobbers.

So what is there to say?

Plenty, as it turns out.

Deliver one of these lines at just the right time, and you can knock your buddy down a peg right in their moment of glory.

- "Even a broken clock is right twice a day. And even a sh*tty fisherman catches something eventually."
- "Nice catch. I think it was already dead when you reeled it in."
- "There are a lot of smart fish in this lake — you obviously found the dumb one."
- "Hope someone took a picture. It might be the last time you have that much hair."
- "Congrats on your first — and last — catch. Might as well hang up the net."
- "Let me take a picture. I want to document the luckiest moment in fishing history."

- "Like a blind squirrel finding a nut... you found a fish. Incredible."
- "So this is where I pretend to be impressed, right?"
- "You didn't catch that fish. It swam up and surrendered."
- "Can't wait to hear the exaggerated story of this catch every year until we die."
- "If you brag about this fish one more time, you're swimming back to shore."

- "So now you've got one fish… and $5,000 worth of gear to thank for it."

TIPS FOR WINNING THE BANTER WAR

Having a bunch of good lines in your back pocket is a great start in the banter war. We've loaded this chapter with some options, and with time and experience, you'll come up with plenty more of your own.

But good lines alone aren't enough. You also need a strategy — an overall approach to talking sh*t that guarantees you rise above your fishing buddies as the undisputed king of the put-downs.

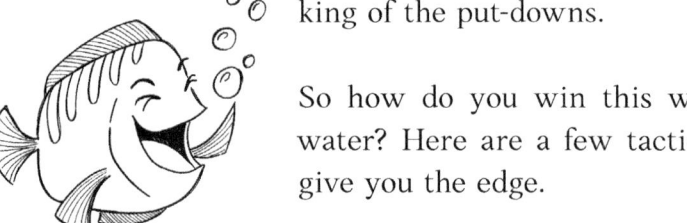

So how do you win this war on the water? Here are a few tactical tips to give you the edge.

Silence can be golden.

Believe it or not, one of the best strategies for talking sh*t is to talk less. If you run your mouth nonstop, eventually you'll say something dumb that undermines the good stuff. Let the other guys dig their own hole — then hit them with a perfectly timed line. The art of the pause is just as important as the line itself.

Know when to get personal.

The holy grail of trash talk is making a personal jab without actually pi**ing someone off. Timing is everything. Making fun of someone's ex-wife the day after the divorce? Too soon. Making the same joke a year later? Fair game.

Know your audience — and know when to pull the trigger.

Chumming: The (usually illegal) act of dumping bait into the water to attract fish. Not to be confused with spilling your Cheetos and beef jerky.

Master the comeback.

You can't rehearse comebacks in advance — sh*t talking is a live sport. You've got to be ready to absorb a hit and fire right back. The more you practice, the better your instincts will be. Deflect, twist, redirect — whatever it takes to turn their punchline into your punchline.

Pay attention.

You never know when someone's going to hand you a perfect insult setup without realizing it. Did they pack on a few pounds since last season? Blow a paycheck on gear they clearly don't know how to use? That's gold. Make a mental note — and save it for the perfect moment. Timing is everything.

What would fishing be without talking sh*t?

Boring, that's what.

Okay, fishing is still boring half the time — but at least trash talking makes the slow parts worth sitting through. So break out some of these lines during your next outing and see which ones hit the hardest. Don't hold back — your friends sure won't. They're just waiting for a chance to return fire... and you should be too.

FISHING GEAR
YOU TOTALLY NEED
(BUT DEFINITELY DON'T)

4

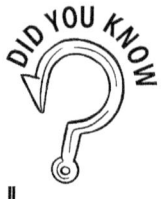

The word *angler* originally referred to someone fishing with a hook. Now it just means someone who wastes all their weekends and money.

In its purest form, fishing is a beautiful battle between man and (aquatic) beast. Armed with little more than a rod, a line, and a bit of bait, the human must figure out just the right place and time to present an offer the fish can't refuse. Then — once the hook is set — the fight begins. Line tension. Steady reeling. Tactics versus instinct.

This is how the game has been played for centuries.

Not anymore.

Today's angler hits the water with more tech than the Starship Enterprise. What was once a primal contest has become a high-priced gear parade. Capitalism took the simplicity of man-versus-fish and turned it into man-with-$2,000-worth-of-gadgets-versus-still-no-fish.

Because surely, with all this innovation and investment, everyone's catching fish hand over fist — right?

Well... that's where it gets interesting.

Somehow, despite dumping a small fortune into sonar, apps, carbon-fiber rods, and enough tackle to open a shop, the average fisherman still heads home with an empty cooler.

Where did it all go wrong?

Since when did throwing a pile of money at a problem not solve it?

This chapter is dedicated to all the gear you "totally need." And by "need," we mean: you think you do.

The fish? They're living just fine—laughing their scaly asses off while you flail around with $2,000 worth of tech that still can't catch a bite.

Drag: A reel setting that helps you land a big one. Also describes your friend who won't shut up about barometric pressure.

If you're thinking rationally, there's absolutely no reason to go overboard with rod and reel upgrades. These are basic, time-tested tools. The rod just guides the line out toward the water, and the reel brings it back in. That's it. That's the job.

Who in their right mind would spend hundreds — or thousands — of dollars on something that simple?

Idiots, that's who.

People who believe they can *buy* their way to fishing glory, despite centuries of proof that fishing success has almost nothing to do with price tags. If you've ever doubted the power of marketing, just look at the ridiculous names printed on modern fishing gear.

There's a sucker born every minute — and most of them are lined up at the local tackle shop, credit card in hand.

If this is starting to feel a little too familiar, you might've been one of them.

Is your rod called the "Lip Ripper 5000"? Does your reel proudly bear the name "White Lightning" or "Spin Master 7000"?

We've got bad news: You might be a sucker.

Why does adding a big number to a fishing product instantly make it seem more legit? Nobody knows. But apparently, four digits = elite. Never mind that "1" or "2" would do just fine for most people. We can only assume that any day now, someone will launch the "Stick of Death 1,000,000."

And when a company finally slaps the word "Infinity" on a reel? They might as well start printing their own money.

AN IRRESISTIBLE LURE

To be fair, it's at least *understandable* why a fisherman might become obsessed with lures. After all, this is the part of your gear that actually gets presented to the fish — it's the business end of the operation. So it makes sense to want a good one.

But somewhere along the way, reason flies out the window.

What starts as a quick trip to the tackle shop turns into a $200 therapy session. Before you know it, you're buying extra tackle boxes just to store your emotional baggage — disguised as soft plastics and shiny crankbaits.

Eventually, your lure collection outnumbers your actual fish caught by about 10 to 1. And your wife wants to know why you can't afford to go on vacation this year. You try to explain that the new lures are an *investment*. She does not agree.

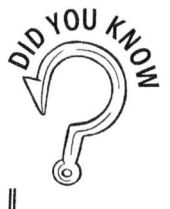

Fly fishing dates back to the 2nd century. You've probably got lures in your tackle box that are just as old.

There are two things that make this whole lure obsession especially ridiculous.

First:

You almost definitely already *own* the lure you're about to buy. It's in there — buried under 50 others you've never used. You just forgot.

But hey, at least you're not wasting that money on something frivolous.

Oh wait — yes, you are.

Second:

You don't even *use* most of them.

Roughly 95% of the lures you buy never touch the water. They sit in the tackle box looking fresh and expensive, trip after trip. You swear you'll try them next time — or the time after that. Or when the moon phase is right. Meanwhile, you fall back on the same three old lures that haven't worked since the '90s.

What's the definition of insanity again? Doing the same thing over and over while expecting different results.

So just remember: every time you tie on that same tired lure and come home empty-handed, you're confirming what your fishing buddies already suspect — you're crazy.

Barbless hook: A hook that slides right out of a fish's mouth — but somehow won't come out of your thumb.

THAT BEAUTIFUL BOAT

Ah, the boat.

Perhaps the most unnecessary, overhyped, and undeniably expensive piece of fishing equipment on the market. Don't think it's unnecessary? Or overpriced? Let's take a closer look.

First — unnecessary.

Every time you head to the boat launch to slide your pride and joy into the water, who do you pass? That's right — people fishing from the shore.

Those same casts you're lobbing from your $40K fiberglass throne? They can do them from a $20 folding chair on the bank.

In fact, it could be argued that the shore fishers are having a better time. No boat ramp chaos. No trailer reversing at weird angles. No batteries, no bilge pumps, no panic when the motor won't start. They just walk up to the water, toss in a line, and hope for the best.

Are they catching loads of fish? No.

But let's be honest—you aren't either. And if you skipped the boat altogether, you'd still have your sanity—and a much healthier bank account.

Let's talk numbers.

It's easy to drop $30,000 to $50,000 on a fishing boat. Think about that for a second. How much did you spend on your last car—you know, the thing you actually use *every day*?

Let's say you spent $40K on both.

Your car? You use it constantly. It gets you places. It justifies itself.

Your boat? You might use it... what? Ten times a year?

Five?

God forbid—once?

And just to twist the knife, you might even be paying monthly storage fees for that glorified sun lounger. Brutal.

Between the price, the hassle, and the fact that fishing doesn't actually require a boat, this whole "investment" starts to look pretty absurd.

With the money you'd save by skipping the boat, you could hire a guide, take a masterclass, or bribe the fish directly.

Hell, you could finally pay someone to teach you how to fish properly. Now there's a wild idea.

Sound travels five times faster underwater than through the air. The fish heard you coming before you even parked the truck.

CLOTHING GONE WRONG

In a hobby like golf, you're basically required to wear the uniform. Sure, golf clothes are arbitrary and often look ridiculous — but if you want to play, you've got to wear the silly pants.

Fishing, on the other hand, there's no such rules. You can wear literally anything. Pajama pants. Old concert tees. Flip-flops from 1998. There's no dress code.

So, naturally, you'd think fishermen don't waste money on "fishing clothes." They just wear whatever's in the laundry pile, right?

Wrong.

Somehow, despite already blowing their budget on rods, reels, and overpriced tackle, many fishermen still fall into the trap — and spend big on "technical" fishing apparel.

Fishing garments come in all kinds of styles.
All of them unnecessary.
Most of them embarrassing.
And almost all of them loaded with pockets.
So. Many. Pockets.

How many things do you really need to carry while standing waist-deep in water, waving a stick around? What's in all those pockets? Snacks? Regret?

And to justify selling you overpriced gear, the companies come up with all kinds of techy-sounding features:

- **"Moisture-wicking."**
- **"Quick-dry."**
- **"Anti-chafe."**

(Which sounds like a personal issue, but okay.)

Shirts, pants, gloves, sunglasses, neck gaiters — it's all part of the fishing fashion arms race. Honestly, the only thing missing from the pro shop is a place to buy a personality.

Tackle box: A portable shrine to your failure. Also home to that sandwich you forgot about last September.

Will any of this gear actually make you a better fisherman? Absolutely not.

You could cover yourself head-to-toe in moisture-wicking miracle fabric and still go home empty-handed. All this gear does is make sure your wallet comes back from the trip just as empty as your cooler.

THE CAST OF FISHING CHARACTERS (A.K.A. PEOPLE YOU'LL REGRET INVITING) 5

Fishing attracts all kinds.

The personalities you meet out on the water are as unpredictable and varied as the fish beneath the surface.

Sometimes, you'll willingly bring these characters along with you. Other times, they just *appear*—and once they're in your orbit, you can't shake them.

Like it or not, your most memorable fishing moments often have nothing to do with actual fishing. They're about the people. The weirdos. The legends. The walking disasters. That's what this chapter is all about.

What follows is a collection of fishing profiles. A deep dive into the characters that every angler has encountered at some point in this ridiculous hobby.

As you read, you'll start mentally sorting your own fishing buddies into these categories.

And yes, that one guy you swore you'd never invite again? He's in here.
And let's be honest—you're going to invite him next time anyway.

THE GEARHEAD

This might be the easiest fishing character to spot — and he doesn't even have to get out of his truck. The gleaming $100,000 pickup hauling a $50,000 bass boat tells you everything you need to know. This is a guy who spends way more time *working* to afford his toys than actually *using* them.

Of course, the gear obsession doesn't stop with the truck and boat. Once the boat hits the water, it's like watching a mobile pro shop unload itself.

Out come the ten tackle boxes, the electronic gadgets, the precision-organized gear pouches, and the rods named after apex predators.

You'd think he was prepping for a televised tournament.

But he's just here... to catch nothing, quietly and expensively.

Live well: A compartment for holding your catch until you head home. On your boat, it's more of a wet storage bin.

Want to have a good laugh? Watch what happens when The Gearhead actually gets a bite. That's when the show starts. Not because he'll display expert technique — far from it.

The entertainment comes from the *panic*.
That moment when he realizes he has to actually *catch a fish* with all the expensive toys he maxed out his credit card to buy.

Odds are, when the line finally tugs, he's mid-adjustment on his GoPro mount — trying to get the perfect angle for his YouTube channel (with 11 followers, mostly bots). Or he's hunched over his phone, tapping through a GPS app to geolocate his boat onto the last known position of a fish that was already caught and eaten two hours ago.

They say even the worst day fishing is better than the best day working.
But when The Gearhead's around, you might start missing your cubicle.
At least *that* doesn't beep every 30 seconds and require Bluetooth syncing.

THE TALL-TALE SPINNER

Okay — every fisherman tells a few lies. It comes with the territory.
How do you know a fisherman is lying?
His lips are moving.
Yeah, it's an old joke. But it still holds water.

So, what makes the Tall-Tale Spinner stand out?
It's the sheer scale of the lies. The drama. The details. The absolute detachment from reality.

Your average fisherman might stretch the truth a little.
That 16-inch bass? Let's call it 18.
Two pounds? More like three, easy.
We all do it. That's standard lake math.

But the Tall-Tale Spinner goes *way* beyond that. He doesn't just exaggerate — he invents. Full-blown fish fiction. Despite coming back with an empty stringer, he'll tell you about the "absolute monster" he pulled in... and then "mercifully" released. Out of the goodness of his heart. Because he's just that humble.
Fortunately, there's a dead giveaway when you're dealing with a classic Tall-Tale Spinner.

Every one of his stories starts with the same line:

"You'll never believe this happened, but..."
And the thing is...
He's right.
You *won't* believe it.
Because it didn't happen.

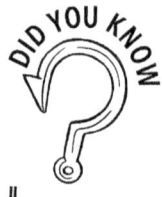

> Fish don't feel pain the same way humans do. Not that it matters — your bad casting hasn't hurt anything anyway.

THE BEER FISHER

Beer is the unofficial — official drink of fishermen everywhere.

Some folks go out on the lake to catch fish.

Most go out just to drink beer somewhere more socially acceptable than their couch.

Think about it:

- "I spent all day Saturday drinking beers alone at home."
  = Sad. Possibly worrying.

- "I spent all day Saturday on the lake having a few cold ones — even though I didn't catch a thing."
  = Awesome. Valid. Therapeutic.

The Beer Fisher is in it for one thing and one thing only: the beers. That's it. That's the mission.

He's not complicated. He's not focused. He's probably not even fully aware there are fish in this lake. But he *is* interesting — and, most of the time, highly entertaining.

Of course, if he's on your boat, be prepared to make regular trips to shore for "pit stops." The man's bladder has the stamina of a fruit fly. So there's that.

Spend a day with The Beer Fisher, and your own quest for the big one will start to feel... kind of silly. Pointless, even. Because honestly — who cares if you catch anything? You're having a great time.

Artificial lure: A fake bait designed to trick a fish. Kind of like your online dating profile.

You'll hear some stories. One might even be true. And you'll laugh a lot — whether it's with him or at him depends on the beer-to-fish ratio. It's hard to find much fault in a day spent with this guy. You won't come away a better fisherman, but you *will* come away buzzed, sunburned, and smiling. And really, that's kind of the whole point.

THE KNOW-IT-ALL

Remember how we said fishing with The Beer Fisher makes for a great day on the lake? Yeah... this next guy is the opposite of that.

Plain and simple, fishing with The Know-It-All sucks. Out of all the characters in this chapter, this is the one to avoid at all costs.

Fishing with him is like sitting next to the kid in class who always had their hand in the air. Answering every question. Correcting your notes. Explaining why your backpack wasn't "ergonomic." It's exhausting.

And the Know-It-All doesn't wait until you hit the water to start his act.

Nope — he gets going on the drive in.

By the time you reach the lake, you'll already know all about how the day's weather is affecting fish migration. Or moon cycles. Or barometric pressure. Or some other nonsense he picked up from a half-read forum post.

You won't ask questions. He'll still give you answers.

Once you're out on the water, he'll make it clear that everyone else is doing it wrong.

Wrong gear. Wrong bait. Wrong spots.

But don't worry—you're with *him*.

And he'll confidently steer you to the exact coordinates of fishing nirvana.

Then... nothing. Total silence from the fish.

Despite having a self-proclaimed rod-and-reel genius onboard, you'll be skunked.

Was he wrong? Absolutely not.

That's when the excuses begin.

The weather changed.

The lake is overfished.

The wind shifted, the moon is off, Mercury's in retrograde.

Whatever it takes.

Because if there's one thing the Know-It-All knows for sure? It's that the problem is **never** him.

Structure: Underwater cover where fish like to hide. Also something your life is completely lacking.

THE SILENT ONE

This person says almost nothing.

And we don't mean "quiet and chill." We mean total silence. From the moment you pick them up to the moment you drop them off.

Doesn't matter how many jokes you crack, how many stories you tell, or how many beers you offer — this person is not interested in participating.

You start to wonder if they're even having a good time.

Are they mad at you?
Are they going through something?
Are they just super focused?

You'll never know. They're not going to tell you.
The Silent One is not there to entertain, emote, or connect. They're there to fish.
Or possibly just... stare at water and think about the futility of existence.

Either way, they're not saying a damn thing.

On the plus side, they're probably not judging you — because they've tuned out the entire universe.

THE ONE-CAST WONDER

This next character is both endearing *and* infuriating — sometimes at the exact same moment.

He's the guy who shows up late, barely glances at his gear, casually flicks his line into the water, and... **bam.**

The big one's in the net in less time than it took you to open your tackle box.

How does he do it?
No one knows.
He doesn't even know.

You'd think it was beginner's luck — except it keeps happening.
Every. Damn. Time.

Trip after trip, the One-Cast Wonder is the first to catch a fish. And not just any fish — it's often the biggest one of the day.

Sometimes he stays humble.
Other times? Not so much.

That's when you'll hear lines like:
"The fish don't like it when you try too hard."

Thanks, guru. Tell that to the rest of us still retying our third lure while you're sipping a beer and basking in glory.
He doesn't know why he's good.

You don't know why he's good.
But he *is* good. And you *hate* that he is.

Some lakes are seeing declining fish populations thanks to overfishing from social media bragging. Congrats—your Instagram post hurt the ecosystem.

THE BEER-DRINKING PHILOSOPHER

A close cousin of the Beer Fisher, this guy also drinks plenty of beer—but along with the beer comes a steady stream of deep thoughts.

We're talking Thoreau in a boat.

He's not here to catch fish.

In fact, he might not even bring a rod.

He just wants to drink, talk about life, drink some more, and maybe ask you if fish have souls.

Spending a day with the Beer-Drinking Philosopher follows a very specific bell curve of enjoyment:

- **Annoying at first**—you're trying to focus while he's wondering if we're *all* just bait in the cosmic tackle box.

- **Surprisingly entertaining midway through**—a few beers in, his weird theories start to sound almost profound.

- **Exhausting by the end**—he's four hours deep into a monologue about "what fishing really *means*," and you'd give anything for a mute button.

By the time you head back to shore, you'll feel like you've just completed a full semester of drunk philosophy—with no credits and no fish to show for it.

THE STORYTELLER

Fishermen like to talk. That much is clear by now. And honestly, that's part of the charm — spending a day on the water, shooting the breeze, letting go of stress, and catching up with your buddies.

But The Storyteller doesn't tell the right kind of stories.

These aren't the fun, laid-back, casual lake chats. These are the kind of stories you'd walk away from at a party. Except here... you're stuck. On a boat. With nowhere to go.

He'll tell you everything about his ex-girlfriends. All seven of them. In excruciating detail. He'll take you on a deep dive into high school drama — even though you all graduated 20 years ago. And don't get him started on office politics. Or his recurring knee pain. Or the guy who cut him off in traffic three years ago.

The worst part?
He thinks he's *great* at telling stories.
He's not.

But he'll keep talking — start to finish, no breaks, no self-awareness. Because The Storyteller doesn't need an audience. He just needs someone who *can't jump out of the boat.*

THE FASHIONABLE GEAR JUNKIE

Sure, plenty of fishermen have a lot of gear. That's normal. This guy, however, takes it to a new level — buying gear specifically for the look.

Function? Optional.
Fashion? Mandatory.

He doesn't just want to catch fish — he wants to look incredible doing it.

Is this a fishing trip or a catalog shoot for Outdoor Vogue?

Match the hatch: A strategy where you match your bait to what's naturally hatching. Or just wing it and pretend you knew it was mayfly season.

The particularly annoying thing about the Fashionable Gear Junkie is that he wants you to notice his ridiculous get-up.

It's not enough for you to focus on your own fishing and let him quietly cosplay as "Tactical Trout Guy." Nope — he's in your face, angling for compliments harder than he's angling for fish.

On one hand, you don't want to give him the satisfaction. On the other, you're *dying* to tell him how ridiculous he looks — and how many mortgage payments he's blown just to match his shirt to his lure.

Tough call.

If there's any silver lining to fishing with this peacock, it's this: he's a terrible fisherman.

Without fail, this guy sucks at catching fish. He's spent so much time, money, and energy prepping for his imaginary photo shoot, there's nothing left for actually learning how to fish.

But hey — at least he looks fantastic doing nothing.

TAKING A LOOK IN THE MIRROR

We know what you're thinking:
"These profiles are funny, but I don't actually know anyone like that."

Here's the bad news — **if none of these characters sound familiar, it's because you're one of them.**

Maybe two of them.
Maybe *all* of them on a really rough day.

Don't feel bad.
Nobody had the heart to tell you before now.
So it fell to us to break the news.

Go back. Re-read the profiles.
Figure out which role you've been playing out there on the water all these years.

And then — either change your ways...
Or fully embrace being the same lovable, annoying bastard you've always been.

THE PSYCHOLOGY OF THE FISHERMAN

6

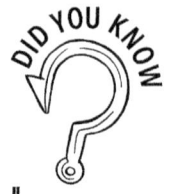

> The average boat owner spends more time maintaining their boat than actually using it. But hey, it looks great sitting in your driveway.

To hear fishermen tell it, fishing—*or angling*, if you're feeling fancy—is one of the greatest hobbies on Earth. They'll wax poetic about the primal battle between man and fish, the serenity of nature, the beauty of silence, the *zen* of the wait.

To the outsider? It all sounds like a steaming pile of bullsh*t.

Because the actual experience of fishing? Let's just say it doesn't always align with the legend.

To most observers, it seems like a frustrating, expensive, mosquito-filled waste of time. If there's some kind of enlightenment to be found while staring at a bobber for six hours straight, it's hiding better than the fish. It's sure hard to see where it is hiding.

But maybe we're being too harsh. (*Probably not.*)

Let's take a closer look at the psychology of the fisherman. Maybe—*just maybe*—we'll uncover the truth about what keeps these poor suckers coming back to the lake again and again.

HOOKED ON THERAPY

One of the most common defenses of fishing — at least from people who love it — is that it's therapeutic. It's marketed as relaxation in its purest form. You breathe in the fresh air, take in the silence, and let your worries melt away.

Yeah. Right.

Anyone who has actually spent five minutes with a fisherman knows that's nonsense.

Sure, they might start off calm.

But give it 30 minutes without a bite and that tranquility goes straight out the window.

It begins innocently enough —
"Man, I thought there'd be more action today."
Still relaxed. But you can feel the mood shifting.

Give it another hour. No bites. No nibbles.
Now we're into the irritation phase:
"There are too many damn people on this lake."
"Why are those kids throwing rocks? They're scaring the fish!"

By the time the sun sets and the boat is back on the trailer, any notion of this being a "therapeutic escape" has long since drowned. Coolers are being slammed shut. Rods are being thrown in the back of the truck like they personally failed. Everyone else in the parking lot is in the way.

And suddenly, Monday at the office doesn't seem like such a bad deal after all.

Still think fishing is relaxing?

Then answer one simple question:
If fishing is so therapeutic... why do fishermen need to drink so much damn beer to get through it?

THE ETERNAL OPTIMIST

Not everyone who goes fishing is bitter and jaded. (*Although it's a pretty common affliction on the water.*)

Some people remain positive — *relentlessly* positive — about this hobby, despite mounting evidence that such an attitude is wildly misplaced.

Backlash: When your line tangles into a mess. Always followed by four-letter words and silent rage.

At some point, optimism stops being charming and slides into full-blown delusion.

Optimism is showing up to a brand-new lake for the first time and thinking,
"This is the day. I'm gonna slay it."
You've got no proof otherwise.
You saw someone post a decent haul on Facebook.
Why couldn't it be you?

Delusion is showing up to that *same* lake for the tenth week in a row, confident it's finally going to happen — despite catching absolutely nothing on the previous nine trips.

At this point, nature is trying to teach you a lesson. You're just refusing to learn.

No matter how many different lures you fling into the abyss, no matter how much expensive gear you add to your setup, you're not catching anything.

And yet...
you smile.
You hope.
You believe.

And honestly? That's kind of beautiful.

Completely detached from reality, yes — but beautiful all the same.

 Salmon return to the exact stream where they were born when it's time to spawn. Yet somehow you can't find your car in the supermarket parking lot.

FEEDING INSECURITIES THROUGH COMPETITION

Fishing isn't supposed to be a competitive activity. The battle is meant to be between you and the fish — not you and every other guy on the lake.

But we're human. And humans turn everything into a competition.

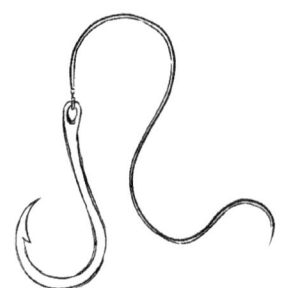

For some fishermen — especially those nursing fragile egos — fishing is just another way to feel better by trying to look better than someone else. The underlying psychology of the competitive fisherman is as sad as it is desperate.

He's just searching for something—*anything*—to feel good about. Even if it means dragging everyone else down along the way.

How do fishermen compare themselves?
Any way they can:

- Who can cast the farthest?

- Who has the biggest boat?

- Who caught the biggest fish?
  (Notice a certain... size obsession here? Hmmm.)

We've already established that fishing as therapy is a stretch. But it *is* a great way to expose insecurities in high definition.

Will winning the day's unofficial competition heal anything? Nope.

This guy doesn't need bragging rights.
He needs a therapist.

JUST ONE MORE CAST

This one goes hand-in-hand with Eternal Optimism—but it deserves its own diagnosis. The "One More Cast" fisherman is absolutely convinced that the *next* cast is going to be the one. It'll land perfectly. The lure will glide just right. And the monster fish? It's definitely out there — waiting.

Never mind the fifty before it. Those don't count. But *this* one? This one's special. It's fate. Destiny. The chosen cast.

This isn't just hope — it's delusion. The same kind you see in gamblers hunched over slot machines, swearing the next spin is going to change everything. In fishing, it's the same mindset — just wetter and more expensive.

And sure, you might argue that unlike the gambler, the fisherman isn't wasting money with every cast.

But aren't they?
Bait and lures aren't free.
Gas costs money.
Boats cost *way* too much.
And don't forget the time — time that could've been spent working, parenting, sleeping, or literally doing anything useful.

But hey — just one more cast.
That'll fix everything.
Totally.

Wind knots: Tangles you blame on the breeze. (Even though everyone knows you just suck at casting.)

SEEKING CONTROL

It's hard to find a sense of control in the world. Everything feels like it's spinning just out of reach, no matter how tightly you try to hold on.

Surely, within a quiet (supposedly peaceful) hobby like fishing, some control can finally be enjoyed.

Right?

And so, with that hope in mind, certain fishermen start obsessing over every last detail of the process.

They chart their fishing locations.
They log which lures they used, what the weather was like, the water temp, the moon phase, the humidity, barometric pressure — maybe even their horoscope.
It's part science experiment, part control-freak therapy session.

Sometimes it's about trying to win. Sometimes it's just about calming the noise in their heads. Control feels like a warm, comforting blanket in a disordered world.

But it never works.

The notebook ends up soaked.
The tackle box gets stolen.
The lucky lure vanishes to the bottom of the lake.

The fisherman seeking total control is destined to fail.

Because this is fishing. And fishing laughs at your spreadsheets.

ARGUMENTS FALLING LIKE WATER THROUGH THE NET

So, after looking at the psychology of the fisherman from a few different angles…

Where does that leave us?

Not very far.

None of the arguments really hold up. Not the therapy angle. Not the "zen peace of nature" nonsense. Not the obsession with gear or competition or control.

Fishing might just be what we thought it was all along: An overrated, time-consuming, money-burning hobby for people who can't sit still and aren't ready to admit they're bored.

But that's not going to stop anyone.

They'll be back next weekend.
Rod in hand.
Cooler full.
Hope irrationally intact.

Because let's be real — golfers need something to do when the course is closed.

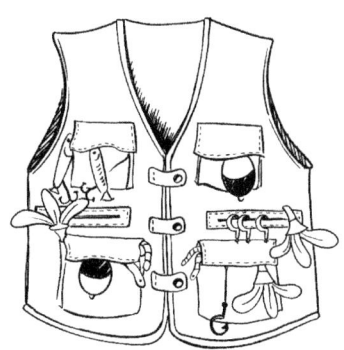

THE FISH ARE LAUGHING AT YOU

7

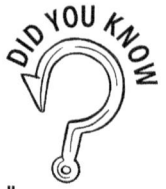

Fish can get "hook shy" after being caught and released. If only you had the same instinct around fast food.

From the perspective of the fish, this sport that so many humans take so seriously must look completely ridiculous.

"What are those people doing up there? Don't they know we can see them? And since when do worms just float through the water like that? They aren't even trying."

Sure, humans win occasionally. Every now and then, one of us gets yanked into the sky and a guy in cargo shorts cheers like he just won the Super Bowl.

But let's keep it in perspective:
Catching one fish out of thousands in a lake and declaring yourself a master angler?
That's like hitting a bird with your car and calling yourself a skilled hunter.

Most of the time, the fish are kicking our collective ass.
They see the lure, shrug, and swim away.
They hear the motor, the music, the cooler lid slamming shut — and decide they're good, thanks.
We spend hours prepping, casting, and retying knots...
And they spend seconds ignoring us.

THOUGHTS FROM THE DEEP

Fish can't talk. (At least... we don't think they can.)

Who knows what's really going on down there while we're up on the surface, fumbling around with gadgets, gizmos, and $20 glittery lures?

Now, obviously, no one has ever *actually* interviewed a fish. So writing an entire section based on what fish *might* be saying about us?

Totally ridiculous.
Borderline unhinged.

And yet — Here we are.

The following is a list of quotes that
have definitely never been said by real fish.
Probably.
Read at your own risk.

- "Nice cast, genius. That's the same log you've hit three times."
- "Why is the human in the boat screaming? *I'm* the one with a hole in my lip."
- "Do they think this is relaxing? They look *furious* up there."
- "This guy's using ten rods — and still no chance I'm biting."

- "Did you know they have a limit on how many of us they're allowed to catch? The limit should be zero."
- "I bit the hook just to snap the line. Totally worth it."
- "He's wearing $500 worth of gear and still can't catch lunch. Impressive."
- "We're supposed to be scared of these guys? One of them just lost a fish to a duck."
- "Corn? Really? When was the last time you saw corn growing in a lake?"
- "Not touching that bait — but I *am* circling back for the snacks they dropped."
- "If they're trying to sneak up on us, blasting country music isn't helping."
- "Pretty sure his vest has more pockets than brain cells."
- "They should just dip a net in. That shiny thing on a hook? Not fooling anyone."
- "Big guy in camo thinks he's invisible. Buddy, we saw you from across the lake."
- "Don't they have anything better to do than sit around all day holding sticks?"
- "One of them just said, 'It's not about catching the fish.' Then what *is* it about, genius?"

- "If that guy casts one more time, I swear he's going overboard."
- "I'm getting fat off all the snacks these clowns drop overboard. Keep 'em coming."
- "Did you see Steve yank that whole rod into the lake? Legendary."
- "They spend hundreds trying to catch us — and still think *we're* the dumb ones."
- "I'd bite just to end it, but honestly... I think I'd rather watch him suffer."

Jerkbait: A bait that darts back and forth to attract attention. Also your nickname in the group chat.

AN ALLURING DELUSION

In the mind of the fisherman, it's all about the lure.

Find the perfect lure, and the fish won't be able to resist. It's like picking out cologne — get the scent just right, and women will fall at your feet. (Despite your complete lack of personality or any other redeeming qualities.)

Except the cologne doesn't work.
And neither do the fancy lures.

It doesn't matter how much money you drop on it, or how many YouTube reviews you watch—fish don't care. You know what they *do* want? Actual food. Not a shiny chunk of plastic with glitter and googly eyes that looks like it escaped from a child's art project.

Here's the best part: fishermen go to absurd lengths to stay hidden. Whispering in the boat. Wearing muted clothes. Using ultra-thin line that vanishes in water like a ninja. Total stealth mode.

And then, at the end of all that?
They slap on a neon crankbait that looks like a disco ball having a seizure.

Brilliant strategy.

This whole game—humans vs. fish—is just a monument to our own hubris. We parade around with overpriced gear and tactical gadgets, convinced we're engineering geniuses. Meanwhile, the fish barely notice. Or worse—they do notice, and they're laughing as they swim away.

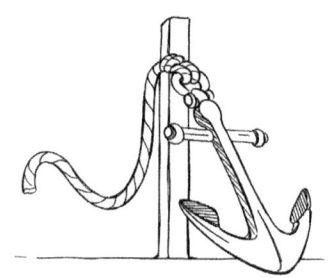

THE ABSURDITY OF CATCH-AND-RELEASE

Of all the bizarre things we've covered in this book — and there have been plenty — nothing tops catch-and-release fishing. Not even close.

Try to put yourself in the fins of an average fish. You're cruising through the water, minding your own business, when suddenly — *POOF* — your buddy just vanishes. Gone. Snatched from above like a scene from a fish horror movie.

Maybe, as a fish, you've seen this before. You know what's up. Every now and then, some unlucky bastard gets yanked out of the water by the sky gods and is never seen again.

But then — what the hell?! — he comes back. Flopping out of the sky and belly-flopping into the lake like nothing ever happened. It's the aquatic version of alien abduction. And now he's swimming around, telling you all about the light, the pain, and the giant human holding him up for Instagram likes.

Now, back to the human perspective — catch-and-release still makes absolutely no sense.

You don't want to eat the fish. You don't want to keep the fish. So... you just traumatize the fish for fun? You stab it in the face, give it a surprise lip piercing, hold it hostage for a selfie, and then toss it back like, *"No hard feelings, right buddy?"*

Seriously — what are we doing?

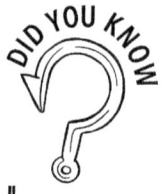

Competitive bass tournaments can have prizes worth a million dollars. Still proud of the five bucks you won off your buddy last weekend?

FISH HAVE MUCH BIGGER PROBLEMS

Here's something that should knock us humans down a peg: fish have way bigger things to worry about than the weirdos bobbing around above them in boats with overpriced rods.

Seriously — on the list of daily threats a fish faces, humans barely crack the top ten.

First off, there are bigger fish. Imagine walking around every day knowing something twice your size might lunge out of nowhere and eat you whole. That's not a fear — it's a lifestyle. No wonder they're not sweating your glittery lure and 12-pound test line.

And if they're not being hunted from below, there's death from above — massive birds diving like missiles out of the sky. That's their version of airstrikes. You think your overpriced crankbait is intimidating after a near-death encounter with a heron?

Then there's the daily grind: finding real food. Not some rubbery neon contraption you've attached to a hook. Actual nutrition. Staying alive out there is a full-time job — and fish aren't quitting just to fall for your nonsense.

The truth is, most fish couldn't care less about you.

You think about them all the time.
You obsess.
You plan.
You spend.

But the fish?
They don't think about you *at all*.

SHOULDN'T WE BE WINNING?

The human brain is massive. Complex. Capable of incredible things.

And yet here we are — getting clowned by fish.

Even with all our intelligence, tools, apps, sonar, and overpriced gadgets, we still regularly get outwitted by creatures that can't remember what happened five minutes ago.

Sure, they've got home-field advantage. They know how to spot a trap. And even when one bites, it'll fight like hell and often still get away — leaving you standing there with your $80 rod and a bruised ego.

But maybe — *maybe* — with more training, more time, and another few thousand bucks sunk into gear, we'll figure it out. Maybe one day, you'll finally stop blowing your weekends and actually catch enough fish to feed your family... and build some glorious, fish-filled memories to pass down for generations.

...

Nah.

Probably not.

THE EVOLUTION OF THE FISHERMAN (IN FOUR PAINFUL STAGES)

8

The best fishing often happens during the so-called "magic hour," just after sunset. That's usually when you're packing up to go home.

The story arc of a fisherman is as predictable as it is sad. We're not saying *every* fisherman follows the exact same path — but let's just say it's a well-worn trail.

Before we begin, an important note:
Yes, we already know *you* think you're the exception.
You're different. Immune.
Sure, the other guys might fall into these stereotypes as they age disgracefully out on the lake, but not you. No way. You've got it all figured out.

That's adorable.
But also? Total bullsh*t. And deep down, you know it.
By the end of this chapter, you'll be sobbing softly to yourself, wondering where it all went wrong.

But don't fight it.
Embrace the somber melancholy that comes with seeing your reality for what it really is. There is healing to be found in the pain.

STAGE ONE — OPTIMISM

Ah, the blissful beginnings...

Much like a kid heading off to school for the first time, the new fisherman is full of wide-eyed excitement. Do they know what they're doing? Absolutely not. But that's part of the charm. It's a brave, dumb new world — and the adventures haven't even begun.

You probably remember this phase. Everything felt possible. You were gonna catch your limit in under an hour — maybe even land a record-breaker. Who knows? Alongside all that optimism came a hefty dose of arrogance. You hadn't been humbled by the fish yet, so you showed up at the lake ready to conquer a hobby that's baffled anglers for generations.

You haven't been corrupted by marketing yet. No overpriced gear, no fancy upgrades. You purchase everything on the cheap — used if you can find it, and if not, inherited from

a relative who gave up on fishing (and life) years ago. Most of it's rusty and dusty, and truth be told, you're not entirely sure how any of it works.

Still, the night before a fishing outing, you drift off dreaming of glory. Big catches. Bigger crowds. People lining up at the dock to snap your picture with the fish of the day. The world is your oyster — or trout, or salmon, or bass.

What could possibly go wrong?

STAGE TWO — OVERCOMPENSATING

The shift from Stage One to Stage Two is slow but steady. One too many fishless trips start to chip away at that bright-eyed optimism. You stay defiant at first — still convinced the fish are coming — but reality begins to gnaw at the edges.

Where the hell are the fish? Why aren't they in your net?

You're still clinging to the dream of becoming an accomplished fisherman — hard. In your mind, you're just a few small tweaks away from that big breakthrough. So, naturally, you start drifting toward the shiny gear lining the walls of the pro shop. If everyone else is buying it, they must know something... right?

Leader: A thicker line near your hook meant to hold during a fight. Spoiler: it won't.

These purchases definitely leave a mark on your credit card statement — but hey, you're finally on the verge of a breakthrough. Right? With thousands of dollars in gear loaded onto the boat and a little experience under your life jacket, the fish must be quivering. This was all worth it... wasn't it?

Much to your shock, nothing really changes. The net is still empty — just more expensively so. You cycle through your shiny collection of lures like a man on the edge. Still nothing. And every now and then, a sliver of doubt creeps in. Maybe this hobby isn't for you. Maybe there's more to it than buying gear and lurking in Reddit forums.

Nah. Those thoughts — sensible as they may be — get crushed like a beer can on the boat floor. You shake it off. Next weekend will be different. It *has* to be.

STAGE THREE — PHILOSOPHY

At some point, there's nothing left to say. Or buy. The results speak for themselves.

You've tried everything you can think of — and everything everyone else has suggested — and the net remains empty. Somehow, some way, the damn net remains empty.

It's at this point the mental gymnastics begin.

You're too deep into this fishing thing to quit — but you also can't keep pretending you're any good at it. So how do you justify pouring more time, money, and pride into a hobby that has produced *exactly zero* evidence of your competence?

Simple:
You get philosophical.
"It was never about the fish," you say.
"It's about the journey. The experience. The time spent outdoors — with others, and with myself."

Sure. Sounds nice.

Catching fish? Just a bonus. An unnecessary one. Allegedly.

We've already covered how the philosophies of fishing don't hold up to even basic scrutiny. But this is all you've got. You're backed into a corner with nowhere left to turn.

So you start droning on to anyone who'll listen about "the virtues of fishing." The lessons it's taught you. The way it's made you a better person — one sh*tty cast at a time.

The fundamental problem with this philosophical stage is that it only runs skin deep. You don't really believe the stuff you're spewing. It's just words — empty ones. Deep down, you still pine to be the fisherman you thought you'd be at the start. The guy on the dock with a crowd gathered around, asking how you did it.

You're trying your hardest to embrace this new perspective on fishing, while also resisting the urge to smash your fist into a tackle box full of lures. It's a confusing time.

Sharks can detect a single drop of blood from a mile away. Just like your spouse can smell another $200 "essential" purchase from the pro shop.

STAGE FOUR — LIFE SENTENCE

At long last, acceptance. The confusion of the philosophical stage can only last so long, and eventually, you settle. You see yourself for what you are as a fisherman.

No, it's not what you wanted.
And no, you'll never truly be happy with it.

There's a difference between acceptance and happiness, after all.

From the outside, you seem more content now. There's still a fire in there somewhere, but it's buried — no longer hot enough to reach the surface.

Other people see you as a "lifer." Someone who's spent enough time failing at this sport to finally let go of the ego.

Fishing just becomes part of you. Is it fun anymore? You're not even sure. It's just what you do. Like brushing your teeth before bed — you do it, then move on. Not what you pictured when this all started, but here you are. Might as well make the most of it while you still can.

At this stage, many fishermen really lean into the lying. Sure, you've been lying all along in one way or another. But now? It's a craft.

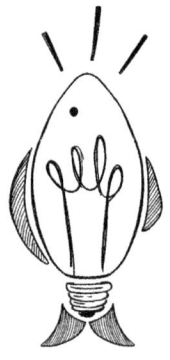

You start telling stories about big fish you never caught — or even saw. You lecture younger anglers about the "good ol' days," when fish used to practically leap into the boat.

Those days never happened.
You've been terrible at this from the start.
But they'll never know.

In a way, the lies let you live the fantasy that never came true. You get to be the hero. Like Superman — completely fictional, but still somehow inspiring.

The story's not real. The hero never existed. But it passes the time on the lake. And it makes the beer go down a little easier.

THE LAKE OF BROKEN DREAMS

Yes, it's a sad story. Watching the wide-eyed optimist who started this "hobby" slowly get broken down by reality is... uncomfortable. Maybe even a little disturbing.

But hey — maybe it's also beautiful.
A tale of growth.
A story about how humans mature and gain perspective as they go through this world.

That would be a wonderful narrative, if it were even slightly true.

For the most part, this is just a story of sh*tty fishing. You suck at this sport and have learned nothing from your journey through the four stages of the fisherman's life cycle.

You'll keep going back to the lake, one weekend after the next, pretending you don't hate yourself and imagining you're still the optimist who first arrived on the shore years ago.

Keep your chin up, champ.

FISHING BUCKET LIST (THAT YOU'LL NEVER COMPLETE) 9

DID YOU KNOW? Fish can detect changes in air pressure — even though they live underwater. Can you detect changes in water pressure?

One of the hallmarks of a great hobby is a long list of goals — or "bucket list" items — you can tick off one at a time as you get better.

A golfer might want to break 100, then 90, then 80. A runner might aim for a sub-4-hour marathon, then 3.5, then qualifying for a famous race like the Boston Marathon.

Fishing has similar targets.

This chapter is all about those bucket list items that countless fishermen keep out in front of them like a dangling carrot. They're the reason you spend so much time and money on such a weird-ass pastime. They fuel the delusion.

Because the passionate angler always thinks they're just one tweak, one purchase, one lucky break away from finally hitting one of these milestones.

There's no real reason to believe that you — or any of your buddies — are ever going to do any of the things below.

But hey. It's nice to dream... right?

CATCH A RECORD FISH

This is usually where it all starts for fishermen who want to *accomplish* something. Once you discover that records exist in the world of fishing, it can become an obsession. You spend hours hunting for obscure records you *might* have a shot at, then plan pilgrimages to the exact lake or river where it was set — just to take your chances.

That sounds fun.
But here's the thing:
You're not breaking any records.

There's a combination of luck, skill, timing, and actual ability required — and you're probably running short on all four.

What actually happens is you waste a ton of time, burn through cash, and come home angrier than when you left — all because you tried to top a record that's lasted for years for a reason.

FISH IN THE OPEN OCEAN

Fishing on a lake is one thing. The water's calm. The fish are small. The whole scene is pretty relaxed. Sure, you still suck at it — but at least it's not intimidating.

Eventually, though, you start thinking bigger.

What if you fished the open ocean?
The *real* stuff. Battling beasts as big as you are, waves crashing over the bow, the kind of drama you see in documentaries and Instagram reels.

Sounds epic.

Also: it's never going to happen.

You'll be seasick before the boat even leaves the harbor.
Reeling in a 100-pound monster with your scrawny arms? Please. You're more likely to fall in and end up *swimming* with the fish than pulling one out.

Bank fishing: Casting from shore instead of a boat. Also what you might have to do to get out of debt after buying too much fishing sh*t.

GO FLY FISHING IN A SCENIC MONTANA RIVER

The state of Montana in the United States is a fantasyland for fishermen. Some of the best fishing in the world happens here.

Crystal-clear rivers. Wide-open skies. Trout practically begging to be caught. It's like a postcard — but wetter.

Fly fishing out there is a dream. A bucket list experience for any self-respecting angler.

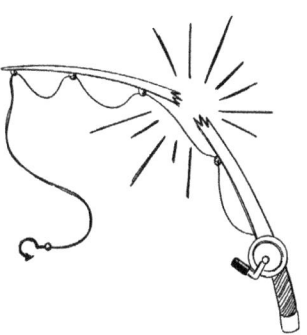

Now stop. Think about it for a second. First off, you don't know how to fly fish.
Hell, you barely know how to *regular* fish.

Gently landing a fly on the surface of a mountain stream while bears watch from the banks? Yeah, no. It's not happening.

The pictures would look great on Instagram, sure — but you'll have to settle for watching someone else rack up the likes.

PARTICIPATE IN A FISHING TOURNAMENT (ON LIVE TV)

Now we're really dreaming big. Competitive fishing takes the hobby to a new level — but hey, why not you? It's not like you need to be an elite athlete. You don't have to be a child prodigy. Just learn how to catch fish, master your technique, put in the hours — and boom, you're on TV.

Or are you?

You can't even outfish your half-drunk buddies at the local lake. But sure, you're going to hang with the pros who've got $50,000 boats, sonar tech, and sponsors stitched across their sleeves.

It might look cool to be on the water, battling the clock to land a monster bass. But let's be honest: the only thing you're landing is snacks — on your couch — while watching guys who actually know what they're doing.

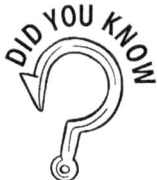

The scent of sunscreen can repel fish. So it's lobster skin or no catch — pick your poison.

TRY ICE FISHING IN SUB-ZERO WEATHER

There is a certain amount of ego involved in planning an ice fishing trip. Oh, fishing when the water's liquid isn't hard enough for you? Cranking up the difficulty by hacking through a frozen slab first is a bold move.

It's also worth asking — even if you could check this bucket list item off... why would you want to? Do you know how cold it has to be for a lake to freeze solid? The weather won't be pleasant, and the fishing will be even worse.

Ice fishing is what people do when they've run out of ideas. Winter rolls in, the restlessness hits, and instead of picking a fun cold-weather activity — like skiing — they decide the best option is to cut a hole in a frozen lake and stare into it. Go figure.

BUILD YOUR OWN ROD

Tired of paying lofty retail prices for your fishing gear? At some point, you might add "build your own rod" to your bucket list — crafting one from natural materials like some kind of off-grid legend.

It's the kind of idea that sounds great in your head. You start Googling, maybe watch a few YouTube tutorials, and suddenly you're convinced this is totally doable.

Then you buy the supplies.

And five minutes into the process, you realize — you're completely out of your depth.

When was the last time you built *anything*? Exactly. Now, instead of a new rod, you've got $500 worth of tools and supplies collecting dust in the man cave.

Some bucket list items are worth clinging to.

This one? Toss it now.

Even if you managed to finish the thing, the experience—and the rod—would fall embarrassingly short of your expectations.

CATCH FISH FROM A KAYAK

Remember how we said that fishing through ice is the move of an overconfident fisherman? Same goes for fishing out of a kayak. Until you've proven you can catch fish from a regular boat, you've got no business sliding into a floating plastic tube and paddling off into the abyss.

A lot more can go wrong in a kayak. In a boat—or on a dock—you've got a pretty good shot at staying dry (assuming you stay sober). In a kayak? All bets are off. One wrong move and you're in the lake—whether you're fighting a fish or just reaching for your last cookie from the cooler.

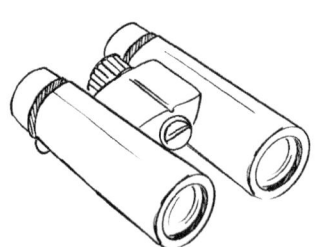

And let's be honest—you're no spring chicken, and you sure as hell aren't Bear Grylls. Have you seen the moves required to get into and out of a kayak? It puts expert-level yoga to shame.

If you do try to check this one off the list, at least you'll be giving everyone at the dock a good laugh—and a story they'll be telling for years.

BECOME A VIRAL SENSATION

Okay—so this one's a bit ambiguous. What exactly counts as a "viral sensation"? Anyone can post a fishing pic or video. But tipping it into *viral* territory? That's a whole different game.

And that's where you'll fall short. To go viral, something has to be unique, exciting, unexpected— and ideally, you'd need to look good while doing it.

More likely, the pictures you and your buddies take on the lake are boring, generic, and downright unflattering. You'll delete them from your cloud before anyone has the chance to see them.

Now—there *is* one possible way you might go viral: by making a complete fool of yourself. Fall out of the boat on video. Fumble your rod into the lake and dive in after it. Hold up your prized catch and watch it flop out of your hands right at the big moment.

People love an epic fail.

And for that brand of fame, you're *highly* qualified!

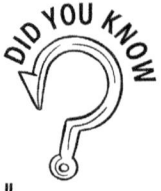

> Some fish use sound to attract mates. And here you are, still updating your Tinder profile hoping for a match.

AN ENDLESS PURSUIT

Would your life suddenly feel complete if you managed to check a few of these off? No. You'd still be you — just with one more story to tell. A story most people will ignore... or assume you made up.

But hey, you're not just in it for the bucket list, right?
This hobby *means* something.
It's bigger than that.

So stick with us for one last chapter.
Let's look at fishing from a different angle — and maybe, just maybe, find something real in the mess of it all.

FINAL CAST: WHAT IT'S *REALLY* ALL ABOUT

10

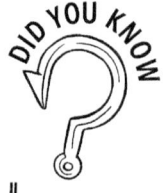

> **Did You Know?** Trout have nearly 360-degree vision. And yet, you still can't spot your own fishing line — through $500 polarized sunglasses.

If you were to ask most people what the goal of fishing is, they'll answer without hesitation: "To catch fish." Seems like an obvious answer to a simple question, right?

It's not.

If the only goal were to catch fish, you (and everyone else) would have quit a long time ago. Any activity where success is rare gets dropped fast. But you're still here and so are millions of others.

Which means catching fish isn't the goal — it's just part of the adventure.

The real goal is immersing yourself in the experience. So, for this final chapter, we're changing gears. Let's take a look at what there actually is to *like* about this ridiculous hobby.

THE POWER OF VARIABLE REWARDS

If you'll allow us, we're going to dip into the world of psychology for a moment.
(Don't panic — we'll keep it brief.)

There's a concept in psychology called *variable reward theory* (or *variable reinforcement*). To oversimplify: humans are more motivated by unpredictable rewards than predictable ones. When a desirable outcome is possible — but not guaranteed — we're more likely to take action and keep trying. Still with us?

That's likely because the anticipation itself is exciting. The result might be enjoyable, sure — but even before that, the *possibility* of the reward is enough to keep us hooked. That combination of hope and unpredictability is a powerful motivator. It's what keeps people doing the same thing over and over again, even when the payoff rarely comes.

Casinos are a perfect example. Most people lose money. Most don't walk away with a jackpot. And yet, they keep playing. Why? Because maybe, just maybe, the next spin is the winner. That tiny chance is addictive.

Fish are constantly peeing into the lake where they live. That might be obvious, but just think about it next time you hop in for a "refreshing" swim.

By now, you can see where this is going. Fishing works exactly the same way. You never know when you'll catch a fish — or if you'll catch one at all. And that uncertainty? That's the magic. You could go home with nothing. Or, you could land the best catch of your life. The endless possibility is what makes it fun. What makes it addictive.

It's entirely possible that this variable-reward system is what you've loved about fishing all along — even if you never quite put it into words. Hopefully, understanding that helps you lean into the madness a little more. At least now you know *why* you keep coming back.

EMBRACING THE WILD RIDE

So, we've established that the unpredictable nature of fishing is a big part of what makes it appealing. You don't know when you're going to catch a fish — or what that fish will look like when (or if) it finally lands in your net.

But the unpredictability goes far beyond just the fish. There's only so much you can control in this sport. The rest? Left up to chance. That might be frustrating, sure — but it's also a big reason why so many people keep coming back for more.

Popper: A surface bait that makes a loud *pop*. Won't catch a thing — but will irritate everyone within 50 feet.

You might do everything right. Pick the right spot. Choose the perfect lure. Nail the cast. You're no expert, but for once, everything aligns. The fish bites. You set the hook perfectly. The fight is on.

And then — the line snaps.

There was nothing you could've done differently. You did it all right, and you still "failed." It's a tough pill to swallow. But it's part of the ride. The sooner you can accept fishing for what it is — not what you *want* it to be — the more fun you'll have out on the water.

You may even start to find a weird kind of joy in the struggle. In the discomfort. The early mornings, the gear malfunctions, the long paddle back to the dock when your motor dies — or runs out of gas. Again.

And then there's the weather. A perfect day on the lake is glorious. But let's be real — that's the exception. Most of the time, it's either too cold, too hot, too windy, or too damn wet.

That's okay. It doesn't have to be perfect.
It *shouldn't* be perfect.
The whole experience gets better because of the mess along the way.

IT'S NOT THE FISH, IT'S THE PEOPLE

At the heart of it all, the truth about fishing is this: it's not about the fish. Sure, the fish might've drawn you to the water in the first place — but they don't have the power to keep you there year after year. Only people can do that.

You might enjoy the occasional solo trip, but this is a hobby made infinitely better with company. Spending time on or near the water with good friends and family — sharing laughs, trading stories, chasing the same dumb fish — is hard to beat.

We've already talked about the trash talk, the zingers, the banter. And yeah, you want to land the best jab of the day. But without your buddies around, none of it would hit the same. The highs, the lows, the long, quiet drives to the lake — it's all part of it. The stories get better with every retelling.

And then, there's sharing it with your kids.

For a kid, heading out onto the lake and trying to catch a fish is a full-blown adventure. Even if you don't land a single bite, that memory might be enough to hook them for life — just like it did for you. They'll want to do it again. And again.

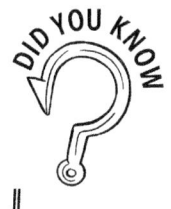

Some fish can survive being frozen and then thawed. Unlike that lasagna you tried to save from last Sunday.

But sometimes, they *will* catch something. And when they do? That look on their face is everything. Worth every cent you spent on gear. Worth every early morning. Worth every frustrating trip where nothing went to plan. Watching your kid — who barely knows what they're doing — reel in a fish and hold it up like a trophy? That's the moment. That's the memory that sticks.

In the end, it's the people who make fishing special. You might show up at the lake alone — but you'll rarely leave that way. You might meet someone new. Make a connection. Or just feel a little more human.

So when you start to wonder if this whole fishing thing is worth it, think about *them*. The people you've met. The ones you haven't yet. That's the reason you'll be back out there next weekend.

And the weekend after that.

So repeat after me...
"It's not about the fish. It's never been about the fish."

Good. Now say it like you mean it.
Louder.

Slower.

Like a man finally accepting the truth he's been running from since he bought his first rod on clearance at Walmart.

It's. Not. About. The. Fish.

Feel better? No? That's okay.
You'll still be back out there next weekend.

CONCLUSION

So, when we add it all up — is fishing really as bad as we've made it out to be in this book?

Well... no. Probably not.

There are good moments. Great ones, even. Sure, they're mixed in with heaps of nonsense, and yeah — plenty of fishermen's behavior is still completely ridiculous.

But there's a reason this sport has stuck around for generations, and why it'll still be here long after you've given up and taken up birdwatching instead.

Fishing isn't perfect.
It eats your weekends.
It drains your wallet.
You often leave the lake with nothing but a sunburn, some mosquito bites, and a quiet sense of personal failure.

But on the right day, when everything clicks — the spot, the cast, the fight — you land something worth remembering. A story you'll tell for years. Maybe even a moment that makes all the garbage worth it.

So don't hang up your rod just yet.

If anything, we hope this book helped you laugh at the absurdity of it all—and maybe reminded you that catching fish is just a small part of why we keep going back.

Thanks for reading. Now get back out there, stay safe—**and try not to screw it up.**

LEAVE A REVIEW

If this book made you laugh—or at least feel slightly better about getting skunked (again)—drop a quick review or a star-rating on Amazon.

It helps other unlucky anglers find the book—and feel a little less alone out there.

No fish? No problem. At least you helped someone else laugh about it.

To leave a review & help spread the word

Printed in Dunstable, United Kingdom